Major Disasters

THE DUST BOWL

BY TRUDY BECKER

WWW.APEXEDITIONS.COM

Copyright © 2024 by Apex Editions, Mendota Heights, MN 55120. All rights reserved. No part of this book may be reproduced or utilized in any form or by any means without written permission from the publisher.

Apex is distributed by North Star Editions:
sales@northstareditions.com | 888-417-0195

Produced for Apex by Red Line Editorial.

Photographs ©: Shutterstock Images, cover, 6–7, 18; George E. Marsh Album/NOAA, 1, 10–11; AP Images, 4–5, 8, 19, 26–27; Arthur Rothstein/Farm Security Administration/Library of Congress, 9, 15, 16–17, 24–25; Dorothea Lange/Farm Security Administration/Library of Congress, 12–13, 20–21, 22–23, 24, 29; iStockphoto, 14

Library of Congress Control Number: 2023910164

ISBN
978-1-63738-756-6 (hardcover)
978-1-63738-799-3 (paperback)
978-1-63738-882-2 (ebook pdf)
978-1-63738-842-6 (hosted ebook)

Printed in the United States of America
Mankato, MN
012024

NOTE TO PARENTS AND EDUCATORS

Apex books are designed to build literacy skills in striving readers. Exciting, high-interest content attracts and holds readers' attention. The text is carefully leveled to allow students to achieve success quickly. Additional features, such as bolded glossary words for difficult terms, help build comprehension.

CHAPTER 1
A DARK CLOUD 4

CHAPTER 2
DUST DISASTER 10

CHAPTER 3
EFFECTS 16

CHAPTER 4
DUST BOWL LESSONS 22

COMPREHENSION QUESTIONS • 28
GLOSSARY • 30
TO LEARN MORE • 31
ABOUT THE AUTHOR • 31
INDEX • 32

CHAPTER 1

A DARK CLOUD

A huge cloud of dust forms in the air. The sky darkens. The dark cloud rises and sweeps across the **Great Plains**.

In the 1930s, many dust storms rose high over the flat land of the Great Plains.

A strong wind whips. The dust covers the dry fields. Everything looks black, and the dirt keeps swirling.

Large dust storms can be bigger than entire towns.

BLACK SUNDAY

A huge dust storm took place on April 14, 1935. It was called Black Sunday. The massive dust cloud was hundreds of miles wide. It traveled up to 60 miles per hour (97 km/h).

FAST FACT

Dust storms were sometimes called "black blizzards."

Dust storms often buried homes and fields. People tried to shovel the dust away.

Soon, the black cloud reaches a town. Families rush inside, but dust pushes through every crack. The people cough and wait for the storm to pass.

Being outside in a dust storm is dangerous. People struggle to see and breathe.

CHAPTER 2

Dust Disaster

In the 1930s, part of the Great Plains faced years of severe dust storms. This area and time became known as the Dust Bowl.

The Great Plains cover 10 US states. Five of these states became part of the Dust Bowl.

The disaster happened for many reasons. Years of **droughts** damaged the land. So did bad farming practices. Too much **grazing** and plowing left the ground bare.

Farmers in the Great Plains cleared land to plant fields.

LOST GRASSES

The Dust Bowl used to be grassland. But farmers dug up **native** grasses. They planted crops like wheat instead. The old grass had deep roots. It held soil in place.

When the ground becomes dry and cracked, many plants can no longer grow.

Without plants to hold it in place, the soil began to blow away. Soon, the good soil that could grow things was gone.

Droughts were especially bad from 1934 to 1935. Many tons of soil blew away.

FAST FACT
Some storms blew dust all the way to the East Coast.

CHAPTER 3

EFFECTS

Drought, soil loss, and dust storms turned the area into a wasteland. Mountains of dust piled up in some places. In others, all the soil blew away.

During the Dust Bowl, parts of the Great Plains looked like a desert.

THE GREAT DEPRESSION

The Dust Bowl happened during the **Great Depression**. Banks across the country failed. Many people became very poor. Farmers struggled to sell their crops. Many went **bankrupt**.

When dust storms hit farms, many plants and animals died. Some people ran out of food.

The dust got into people's lungs. It also killed crops. Thousands of people died. Hundreds of thousands lost their homes or farms.

◀ **People all over the United States struggled to find work and food during the Great Depression.**

Many people became **migrants**. They made long journeys to find new jobs and places to live. They left their homes and land behind.

Dust Bowl migrants often packed their belongings into cars. They drove to other parts of the country.

FAST FACT
During the Dust Bowl, around 2.5 million people left the area.

CHAPTER 4

DUST BOWL LESSONS

The US government worked to help both people and the land. It bought farmers' wheat and animals. It also paid some farmers to stop planting.

Several government programs helped struggling farms make money.

Deep, straight plowing can damage land. Using curved plowing can help.

Some government programs planted new trees and plants. Others helped farmers change how they grew crops. Both helped the soil recover. Access to water improved as well.

In crop rotation, farmers plant different crops each year.

SAVING THE SOIL

Hugh Hammond Bennett helped the US government make plans. His ideas included **crop rotation** and new ways of plowing. Both kept soil healthy. So, Bennett was called the Father of Soil Conservation.

By the 1940s, both the Dust Bowl and the Great Depression had ended. Farms began making money again. The response to the disaster was a success.

FAST FACT
The US government planted more than 200 million trees.

The Shelterbelt Project planted trees near the edges of fields to protect them. By 1945, many fields had recovered.

COMPREHENSION QUESTIONS

Write your answers on a separate piece of paper.

1. Write a few sentences describing why the Dust Bowl happened.

2. If you lived in the Dust Bowl during the 1930s, would you stay or leave? Why?

3. Which area was most affected by the Dust Bowl?

   A. the East Coast
   B. the Great Plains
   C. the Great Depression

4. Why did the government pay farmers not to plant fields?

   A. so the fields could be used to build roads
   B. so the farmers could lose more money
   C. so the land could have time to recover

5. What does **massive** mean in this book?

*The **massive** dust cloud was hundreds of miles wide.*

    A. very big
    B. very heavy
    C. very popular

6. What does **conservation** mean in this book?

*Both kept soil healthy. So, Bennett was called the Father of Soil **Conservation**.*

    A. work to get rid of something
    B. work to keep something safe
    C. work to make something cost more

Answer key on page 32.

GLOSSARY

bankrupt
Unable to pay debts.

crop rotation
Changing the types of crops grown in a field, rather than planting the same crop each year.

droughts
Times of little or no rain.

grazing
Having animals eat grass growing in fields.

Great Depression
A time from 1929 to 1939 when banks failed and many people lacked money or jobs.

Great Plains
A large grassland area that covers parts of the United States and Canada.

migrants
People who move to a new place, often to find work.

native
Originally living in an area.

TO LEARN MORE

BOOKS

Gendell, Megan. *Droughts*. Mendota Heights, MN: Apex Editions, 2023.

Pettiford, Rebecca. *Droughts*. Minneapolis: Bellwether Media, 2020.

Smith, Elliott. *Focus on the Great Depression*. Minneapolis: Lerner Publications, 2023.

ONLINE RESOURCES

Visit **www.apexeditions.com** to find links and resources related to this title.

ABOUT THE AUTHOR

Trudy Becker lives in Minneapolis, Minnesota. She likes exploring new places and loves anything involving books.

B
bankrupt, 18
Bennett, Hugh Hammond, 25
Black Sunday, 7

C
crop rotation, 25
crops, 13, 18–19, 24

D
droughts, 12, 16
dust, 4, 6–7, 9, 15, 16, 19
dust storms, 7–8, 10, 15, 16

F
farmers, 13, 18, 22, 24

G
grazing, 12
Great Depression, 18, 26
Great Plains, 4, 10

M
migrants, 20

S
soil, 13–14, 16, 24–25

U
US government, 22, 24–25, 27

ANSWER KEY:
1. Answers will vary; 2. Answers will vary; 3. B; 4. C; 5. A; 6. B